Islamic Accounting

Steven M. Bragg

AccountingTools®

ISBN 978-1-64221-199-3

For more information about AccountingTools® products, visit our Web site at www.accountingtools.com.

Table of Contents

About the Author

Steven Bragg, CPA, has been the chief financial officer or controller of four companies, as well as a consulting manager at Ernst & Young. He received a master's degree in finance from Bentley College, an MBA from Babson College, and a Bachelor's degree in Economics from the University of Maine. He has been a two-time president of the Colorado Mountain Club, and is an avid alpine skier, mountain biker, and certified master diver. Mr. Bragg resides in Centennial, Colorado. He has written more than 300 books and courses, including *New Controller Guidebook*, *GAAP Guidebook*, and *Payroll Management*.

Steven maintains the accountingtools.com web site, which contains continuing professional education courses, the Accounting Best Practices podcast, and thousands of articles on accounting subjects.

Buy Additional AccountingTools Courses

AccountingTools offers more than 1,500 hours of CPE courses, with concentrations in accounting, auditing, finance, taxation, and ethics. Related courses that you might like include:

- GAAP Guidebook
- International Accounting

Go to accountingtools.com/cpe to view these additional courses.

AccountingTools®

Islamic Accounting

Introduction

This manual covers the unique aspects of Islamic accounting as it is applied to a business. Under Islam, religious concepts and business activities are considered to be closely intertwined, resulting in some accounting practices that are not found elsewhere. Overall, this means that Islamic accounting can be considered the process of recording and reporting business transactions about the extent to which a reporting entity is meeting its financial and social objectives under Islamic law.

Alignment with IFRS

Islamic accounting is very closely aligned with the accounting framework for International Financial Reporting Standards (IFRS). Both systems use double-entry accounting, and largely employ the same types of journal entries. In addition, they all employ the same accrual concepts, such as prepaid expenses, accrued expenses, accrued income, and unearned revenue. These systems also accumulate accounting information in the same manner – through a general ledger that is organized with a chart of accounts. Further, the information in the general ledger flows into a trial balance and from there into a set of financial statements, which are produced after a series of closing entries have been made. In short, someone trained in IFRS accounting would be able to operate an Islamic accounting system in most respects, except for the issues noted in this manual.

Sources of Islamic Law as it Pertains to Accounting

The main source of Islamic law is the Quran; this is the Islamic sacred book, believed to be the word of God as dictated to Muhammad by the archangel Gabriel. The Quran contains 114 units of varying lengths, which are known as suras. These suras address all aspects of human existence, including matters of doctrine, social organization, and legislation. This is the primary source of guidance regarding business activities, but it is also supplemented by the Sunnah, which is the body of traditional social and legal custom and practice of the Islamic community. A further source of guidance is comprised of the judgments of Muslim jurists on matters not specifically covered by the Quran. Together, these three sources form the basis for Islamic law. In aggregate, these sources may be referred to as *Sharia*, which is the entirety of Islamic law, prescribing both religious and secular duties.

The essential issue governing Islamic accounting is the extent to which an Islamic business is to be operated in an ethical manner. Islamic law emphasizes the welfare of the community over that of the individual, and so places an emphasis on investments that help the community. This does not mean that an individual cannot become wealthy through the conduct of business, but recognizes that an excessive degree of inequality within a community is unlikely to benefit society as a whole. In this respect,

Islamic principles tend to mitigate the social and environmental damage that can be caused by unmitigated capitalism.

Islamic law allows the accumulation of wealth, as long as it is put to uses that yield acceptable types of economic development. Acceptable development is oriented toward the improvement of the community, so that wealth is fairly distributed.

Types of Islamic Business Entities

The types of business entities used in an Islamic environment are similar to those used in a purely capitalist society. Sole proprietorships are used, where the owner runs the business and is personally liable for its debts. Several variations on the partnership concept are also used, where the partners share in the profits and losses of the business, and are personally liable for its debts. Limited partnerships are allowed, as is a special form of partnership, known as a *mudaraba*, in which one party provides the capital while the other party provides labor, with both sharing in the profits[1]; the first party is considered to be the financier, while the second party is the working partner. Companies are also used, where the company is a separate legal entity from its shareholders; the shareholders are only liable up to the amount of their investments in the company. The only difference from the company concept in a capitalist society is that preferred shares are not allowed, because they create an earnings inequality among the owners.

Prohibited Activities

Several activities are prohibited under Islamic law. They are as follows:

- *Interest*. The charging or receipt of interest is prohibited. The underlying concept is that one's wealth should not be used to generate interest (which requires no work), which would tend to unduly concentrate wealth and expand the differences between rich and poor.
- *Exploitation*. Paying an unfairly low wage is considered unjust, as is setting excessively high prices. Ideally, wages should be set at a level that supports the dependents of employees, while prices should incorporate the cost of goods and include a fair profit.

Rather than charging interest, an Islamic bank earns income via profit sharing with its customers, thereby directly sharing the risk of generating income with them. This approach forces those with wealth to engage in economic activities, rather than relying on passive income from interest. The result is that, rather than reporting loans receivable on your balance sheet, you would report participations.

---

[1] Current value information is needed for the calculation of shares held in a mudaraba partnership.

The Concept of Zakat

Zakat is one of the Five Pillars of Islam and is a specific form of alms that is obligatory for any Muslim who is in possession of wealth over a certain threshold. Zakat is applicable at a rate of 2.5% of a Muslim's total wealth above a minimum threshold amount (known as Nisab) and is calculated and paid annually. This is not charity, since Zakat is compulsory. Charity is considered to be voluntary.

We just stated that the standard Zakat rate is 2.5%. Actually, it can be higher, depending on the category of wealth. That percentage applies to wealth that is comprised of gold, silver, cattle, and other domestic animals. However, the rate increases to 10% for agricultural and farming produce when the land is irrigated by natural means, but is only 5% if the land is irrigated artificially (since this requires more effort). If the wealth is associated with a mine or a treasure-trove, then the Zakat percentage increases to 20%.

Zakat is payable by all qualifying businesses and individuals. Zakat accounting is targeted at the proper computation and collection of Zakat. The collection of Zakat depends on the country; there is typically a national agency charged with its collection and subsequent disbursement. If you fail to pay Zakat which you owe, you will incur a monetary penalty, and may end up in jail as a defaulter (depending on the country).

The Basis of Zakat

Zakat is paid on the wealth of a business, but only on its "growing" capital, which is defined as its gains on capital assets and inventories. Capital assets are considered to be fixed assets (such as tools and machinery), while inventories include anything that is being made available for resale. More specifically, Zakat is payable on cash, inventory, accounts receivable, and marketable securities, minus any liabilities related to these items. In effect, Zakat is payable on net working capital. The gains on which Zakat is calculated include both realized and unrealized gains, but Zakat payments are only made on realized gains; this is because paying Zakat based on unrealized gains might require you to sell off some assets, which in turn reduces your asset base, possibly reducing your ability to pay more Zakat in the future.

Assets are only subject to Zakat when all of the following conditions are present:

- The asset is possessed and controlled by the owner. For example, a leased asset does not qualify, because you control the asset but do not possess it.
- The asset is growing in value or is expected to do so. As stated earlier, this is assumed to be capital assets and net working capital.
- The asset does not have any debt associated with it. For example, if you purchased an asset for $10,000 and there is an $8,000 loan outstanding against it, then the asset amount subject to Zakat is $2,000.
- The asset has been owned for at least one year.
- The asset exceeds the owner's basic personal and trade needs.

Some additional rules pertaining to the basis of Zakat are as follows:

- *Donated assets.* When a business accepts donations, a Zakat liability is incurred when these assets are sold for cash.
- *Investments.* Any investments classified as trading securities are subject to Zakat, while available-for-sale securities are not.
- *Dividends received.* Dividends received are subject to Zakat.
- *Bad debts.* The amount of Zakat payable on accounts receivable is reduced by any bad debts and a provision for doubtful debts.
- *Prepaid expenses.* Prepaids are not subject to Zakat, since the underlying asset is not fully controlled by the business.
- *Inventory.* Only finished goods are subject to Zakat, since they are in a sellable condition. Raw materials and work-in-process are not subject to Zakat.
- *Payables.* All trade payables are deducted from current assets in order to calculate Zakat.
- *Accrued expenses.* Any liabilities payable within the following year are deductible for calculating Zakat, so all accrued expenses are likely to be deductible.
- *Taxes.* Any taxes paid on the current year's tax can be deducted for Zakat calculation purposes.
- *Fixed assets.* Fixed assets are not subject to Zakat, but Zaat is due on the cash proceeds if a fixed asset is later sold.

Nisab represents the lowest amount that a Muslim must possess to fulfill the Zakat obligation. This amount was established with the equivalence of 87.48 grams of gold or 612.36 grams of silver. These amounts are converted into the local currency, based on the current market prices of gold and silver. However, if a person incurs debt or falls below the Nisab threshold at any point during the year, they must reach and sustain the Nisab for another full year before they are eligible to pay Zakat again.

How to Calculate Zakat

In the preceding sub-section, we covered a number of rules pertaining to the asset base upon which Zakat is to be calculated. More specifically, either the net assets method or the net invested funds method can be used to derive the Zakat base; the calculation appears in the following two exhibits. These methods should produce the same outcome.

Calculation for the Net Assets Method

+	Cash + receivables + finished goods inventory + held for trading investments
-	Accounts payable + accruals + minority interest + equity owned by public entities or NGOs
=	Zakatable base

Calculation for the Invested Funds Method

+	Share capital + reserves + retained earnings + net income + long-term liabilities
-	Net fixed assets + available-for-sale investments + real estate
=	Zakatable base

EXAMPLE

Riffa Furniture has produced the following balance sheet as of the end of its most recent calendar year of operations:

Current Assets		Current Liabilities	
Cash	8,000	Accounts payable	6,000
Accounts receivable	19,000	Accrued expenses	4,000
Finished goods	23,000		10,000
Raw materials	16,000		
	66,000		
		Equity	
Long-Term Assets		Capital	80,000
Fixed assets	20,000	Reserves	36,000
Real estate investments	50,000	Profit	10,000
	136,000		136,000

Riffa's accountant wants to determine the amount of Zakat payable by the company. To do that, he first calculates the aggregate amount of current assets, which is found with the following calculation:

Cash	8,000
Accounts receivable	19,000
Finished goods	23,000
Total current assets	50,000

The accountant then calculates the aggregate amount of the firm's current liabilities, which is found with the following calculation:

Accounts payable	6,000
Accrued expenses	4,000
Total current liabilities	10,000

The net current asset figure resulting from these steps is 40,000 (calculated as 50,000 total current assets – 10,000 total current liabilities). To this figure he adds a donation of 2,000 that the company received recently, and subtracts out 500 relating to obsolete inventory, resulting in a net current asset figure of 41,500.

Finally, the accountant multiplies the adjusted net current asset figure of 41,500 by the 2.5% Zakat rate, to arrive at a Zakat liability of 1,037.50.

The Timing of Zakat Payments

Zakat is paid when a Muslim has possessed the Nisab for a complete lunar year. A lunar year has a duration of about 354 days. However, businesses are more likely to follow the normal calendar (Gregorian) year, which is 365 days. Since the calendar year is longer than the lunar year, a business pays a higher Zakat rate of 2.5775% (calculated as 365 days ÷ 354 days × 2.5%).

Zakat is typically paid in cash. However, it is permissible to pay it with trade goods, especially if the business is short on cash or if such in-kind payments can be of assistance to the targeted beneficiaries.

The Distribution of Zakat

The funds collected from Zakat are distributed to eight categories of people, as specified in the Quran. Depending on the translation, these categories are as follows:

> Alms are meant only for the poor, the needy, those who administer them, those whose hearts need winning over, to free slaves and help those in debt, for God's cause, and for travelers in need.

Responsibility for Zakat Payments

Islamic law states that individuals are the parties that must pay Zakat. In addition, companies may be required to pay Zakat. In the latter case, an organization's net current assets are used as the basis for calculating Zakat. There are four specific instances in which a company is required to pay Zakat, which are as follows:

- The law requires the firm to pay Zakat.
- The firm's bylaws require it to pay Zakat.
- The shareholders pass a resolution calling for the firm to pay Zakat.
- The owners of the firm authorize it to pay Zakat on their behalf.

Note: In a few countries, the amount of Zakat that an individual pays can be deducted as a rebate from their income tax payable.

Accounting for Zakat

Zakat payments made by a business are classified as an expense, while any unpaid Zakat balance is classified as a liability. However, if the firm's shareholders require the business to pay Zakat on their behalf, then these payments are treated as a deduction from their share of the firm's distributable profits. If there are not enough distributable profits to cover the Zakat payments, then the firm records a receivable due from the shareholders for the difference.

Disclosure of Zakat

A business that issues financial statements in accordance with Islamic law should disclose in the accompanying footnotes the method used to calculate the firm's Zakat base, as well as the items included in this calculation. The organization should also reveal whether it pays its portion of the Zakat obligations of its subsidiaries. And, in cases where the entity has not paid Zakat, it should disclose the amount for which the firm is liable.

The Concept of Sukuk

As already noted, it is not permissible under Islamic law to charge interest. This means that a business cannot issue bonds that pay any amount of interest to investors. Instead, a business can issue a *sukuk*, which is an Islamic financial certificate. The issuing business then uses the proceeds from the sukuk issuance to purchase an asset, in which investors have a direct partial ownership interest. In addition, the issuer has an obligation to buy back the sukuk at a future date at its par value. Investors will then receive a portion of the earnings generated by the purchased asset. This type of bond structure means that a sukuk can only be used when identifiable assets are to be purchased with the funds raised; this tends to limit its use to large, carefully-defined capital expenditure projects.

> **Note:** An interesting side issue is that sukuk valuation is based on the value of the assets backing them, while the price of a bond is primarily determined by its credit rating.

Sukuk is generally issued through a *special-purpose vehicle* (SPV). This involves the originator, which is the business that is in need of funding, the intermediary handling the sukuk issue (the SPV), and the investors who will be sukuk holders. It is also possible for the originator to replace the SPV with a trustee, who is responsible for managing the cash flows of the sukuk issuance. The trustee represents the interests of the sukuk holders.

There are multiple types of sukuk arrangements. Consider the following options for how one might be structured:

- *Sukuk istisna*. This is an arrangement in which goods are manufactured while the purchase price is delayed. The manufacturer then issues sukuk certificates, which are ownership interests in the goods that have not yet been produced. Once the goods are delivered, investors will own a portion of these goods. The goods are then sold, and the proceeds distributed to the investors.

- *Sukuk ijarah*. Under this arrangement, the originator transfers assets to an SPV, which then sells sukuk certificates to investors. The investors then have an ownership interest in the transferred assets. The SPV then leases the assets back to the originator. As scheduled lease payments are made, these payments are issued to the various investors.
- *Sukuk mudaraba*. This is a profit-sharing arrangement between investors and the originator, where profits are shared in accordance with a pre-set profit ratio. Investors own the underlying assets.
- *Sukuk musharaka*. This is partnership arrangement in which the parties share in all profits and losses. All parties are entitled to participate in its management, if they choose to do so. Profits are split in accordance with a profit-sharing ratio, while losses are covered in proportion to each investor's capital contribution.

When a sukuk is designated as asset-backed, the investors literally own a share of the specific asset that was bought with their funds. Therefore, even if the originator goes bankrupt, the investors will have rights to the cash flows generated by the acquired asset. When an SPV is involved, it actually holds the acquired asset as a trustee. Under this arrangement, the investors assume any losses if the sukuk asset is impaired. This means that an asset-based sukuk arrangement has the characteristics of an equity holding, rather than a debt investment.

It is also possible to have an asset-based sukuk, where the originator guarantees payment of both the principal and interest. This arrangement essentially replicates a traditional bond sale, since the underlying asset is not being sold to investors. In this case, the investors do not have recourse against the asset, but rather against the originator. Therefore, an asset-based sukuk is oriented toward the creditworthiness of the originator, rather than the risks associated with the underlying asset(s).

When an investor purchases an interest in sukuk, the investment may be classified as held for sale, if the investor intends to only keep the investment for a short period of time. Held for sale investments are reported at their fair market value at the end of each reporting period, where gains and losses are recorded within the unrealized holding gains and losses line item in the income statement. Alternatively, if the investor intends to hold the investment to maturity, then it is classified as held to maturity. Held to maturity investments are recorded at their cost, with gains or losses only recorded upon maturity. Finally, if neither of these investment categories applies to the investor's intentions, then it is classified as available for sale. Available for sale investments are carried on the investor's books at fair value; if there is a change in fair value from period to period, the gain or loss is recorded in a separate component of equity.

When engaged in sukuk transactions, the originator should disclose the following information alongside its financial statements:

- The value of the sukuk
- The percentage acquired from each party
- The type of sukuk
- The party guaranteeing the sukuk and the nature of that guarantee
- The contractual relationship between the originator and the holders of the sukuk
- The classification of sukuk, according to its maturity

EXAMPLE

Haima Construction needs an additional $50 million to pay for the expansion of its operations, and wants to do so by issuing sukuk ijarah. On January 1 of 20X1, Haima creates a special-purpose vehicle and sells its corporate headquarters to the SPV for $50 million. The SPV then sells $50 million sukuk to investors, and holds the Haima headquarters in trust for them. Haima agrees to buy the building back four years later, for $55 million. In the interim, it has leased the building for $2 million per year. In essence, Haima Construction is engaged in a sale and leaseback transaction in order to obtain sufficient cash to fund its growth plans.

From the perspective of the investors, there will be a fixed return of $5 million when Haima eventually repurchases the building, even if the value of the building has declined during the interim. In addition, the investors will be paid their share of the annual $2 million in lease payments, minus any trusteeship and operating expenses incurred by the SPV.

Once Haima enters into this arrangement, it includes the following footnote in its financial statement reporting package:

> On January 1, 20X1, Haima Construction entered into a sukuk financing transaction by selling its corporate headquarters to an SPV for $50 million and then leasing the facility for four years, at an annual lease rate of $2 million. Haima will repurchase the building at the end of the lease term for $55 million. Since Haima retains all of the risks and rewards associated with this transaction, it is accounted for as a financing transaction.

Islamic Financial Statements

The basic set of financial statements is still required under Islamic accounting, which means that a business should produce an income statement, balance sheet, statement of cash flows, and statement of changes in owners' equity. Since Zakat is paid at the end of each year, a business must report the standard set of financial statements at that time, in order to calculate the amount of Zakat owed.

A sample income statement formatted for Islamic accounting appears in the following exhibit. Note the inclusion of a line item for the Zakat payment, which is positioned after net income but before taxes.

Islamic Accounting Income Statement

Revenue	1,000,000
Cost of goods sold	400,000
Gross margin	600,000
Operating expenses	450,000
Net income before **Zakat** and taxes	150,000
Provision for Zakat	3,750
Taxes	29,250
Net income (loss)	117,000

A variation on the income statement is the value-added statement, which focuses on how the funds generated by a business are distributed to its various stakeholders, rather than on how much profit it generates. An example format appears in the next exhibit, where a value-added statement shows how much funding is distributed to employees, owners, charities, the government, and so forth. This format provides a good view of how much a business is contributing back to society.

Islamic Accounting Value-Added Statement

Sources of value-added	
Revenue	50,000
Less: Purchased items	-20,000
	30,000
Distributions	
Beneficiaries (Zakat)	300
Charities	1,500
Employees (wages)	18,000
Government (taxes)	4,500
Investors (dividends)	2,000
Reinvested funds:	
Retained profit	3,700
	30,000

An essential element of Islamic accounting is to state a firm's assets and liabilities at their fair values, since Zakat is calculated from this aggregate amount. This can be accomplished on the balance sheet by stating both the cost and fair value of each line item in a separate column. This format appears in the following exhibit. In this format, fair value is considered to be the amount paid in an orderly transaction between a willing buyer and seller.

Islamic Accounting Balance Sheet

Assets	Cost	Fair Value	Liabilities	Cost	Fair Value
Current assets			**Current liabilities**		
Cash	40,000	40,000	Accounts payable	12,000	11,000
Accounts receivable	80,000	78,000	Salaries payable	5,000	5,000
Unbilled sales	5,000	4,000	Sales received in advance	3,000	3,000
Supplies on hand	3,000	1,000	**Total current liabilities**	20,000	19,000
Prepaid insurance	7,000	7,000			
Prepaid rent	15,000	15,000	Long-term liabilities	10,000	9,000
Total current assets	150,000	145,000	**Total liabilities**	30,000	28,000
Fixed assets	120,000		**Equity at end of period**	200,000	200,000
Accumulated depreciation	-40,000				
Total fixed assets	80,000	95,000	Revaluation reserve	--	12,000
Total assets	230,000	240,000	**Total liabilities & equity**	230,000	240,000

There are several areas in which differences can arise between the reported cost and fair value of an asset or liability. For example, the fair value of a receivable may be less than its reported cost if the recoverable amount is lower. This is also frequently the case with inventories, which may lose value over time. Conversely, there is some chance that the fair value of fixed assets will be higher than their cost, especially in the case of real estate holdings.

The differences between the cost and fair value amounts on the preceding balance sheet are stated in the revaluation reserve, which is required to balance the fair value version of the balance sheet.

A sample statement of cash flows formatted for Islamic accounting appears in the following exhibit. Note the inclusion of a line item for the provision for Zakat, as well as an offsetting line item for Zakat paid. Both items appear within the net cash provided by operating activities section.

Islamic Accounting Statement of Cash Flows

Cash flows from operating activities		
Net income		3,000,000
Adjustments for:		
Depreciation and amortization	125,000	
Provision for losses on accounts receivable	20,000	
Provision for Zakat	165,000	
Zakat paid	-100,000	
		-65,000
Increase in trade receivables	-250,000	
Decrease in inventories	325,000	
Decrease in trade payables	-50,000	
		25,000
Cash generated from operations		3,105,000
Cash flows from investing activities		
Purchase of fixed assets	-500,000	
Proceeds from sale of equipment	35,000	
Net cash used in investing activities		-465,000
Cash flows from financing activities		
Proceeds from issuance of stock	325,000	
Dividends paid	-45,000	
Net cash used in financing activities		280,000
Net increase in cash and cash equivalents		2,920,000
Cash and cash equivalents at beginning of period		2,080,000
Cash and cash equivalents at end of period		5,000,000

A sample statement of changes in owners' equity for Islamic accounting appears in the following exhibit. This is substantially the same format used by businesses reporting the same information under the GAAP or IFRS accounting frameworks.

Islamic Accounting Statement of Changes in Owners' Equity

Description	Paid-Up Capital	Retained Earnings	Total
Balance at 1/1/20X1	28,000,000	2,000,000	30,000,000
Net income	--	2,500,000	2,500,000
Distributed profits	--	-2,000,000	-2,000,000
Balance at 12/31/20X1	28,000,000	2,500,000	30,500,000

If the balance sheet is structured to show the fair value of assets and liabilities, then a revaluation reserve column can be added to the statement of changes in owners' equity. An example appears in the following exhibit, where we assume that the beginning revaluation reserve is 100,000 monetary units, with an additional 200,000 units being added to the reserve in the current year.

Islamic Accounting Statements of Changes in Owners' Equity with Revaluation Reserve

Description	Paid-Up Capital	Retained Earnings	Revaluation Reserve	Total
Balance at 1/1/20X1	28,000,000	2,000,000	100,000	30,100,000
Net income	--	2,500,000		2,500,000
Increase in market value of net assets			200,000	200,000
Distributed profits	--	-2,000,000		-2,000,000
Balance at 12/31/20X1	28,000,000	2,500,000	300,000	30,800,000

A financial statement that is unique to Islamic accounting is the statement of sources and uses of funds in the Zakat and charity funds. This report shows the source of funds assigned to Zakat and how those funds are applied, along with any fund balance remaining at the end of the period. The charity funds referred to in the title of this report are discretionary payments, as opposed to the mandatory Zakat payments. A sample report appears in the following exhibit.

Sample Statement of Sources and Uses of Funds in the Zakat and Charity Funds

Sources of Zakat and charity funds	
Zakat due from the company	1,700,000
Donations	100,000
Total sources	1,800,000
Uses of Zakat and charity funds	
Zakat for the poor and needy	250,000
Zakat for the wayfarer	180,000
Zakat for the heavily indebted and freedom of slaves	120,000
Zakat for new converts to Islam	400,000
Zakat for the cause of Allah	290,000
Zakat collection and distribution to staff (administrative)	120,000
Total uses	1,360,000
Increase (decrease) of sources over uses	440,000
Undistributed Zakat and charity at the beginning of year	60,000
Undistributed Zakat and charity funds at end of year	500,000

In cases where Zakat payments are made directly by the owner of a business, a business should disclose this in the notes accompanying its financial statements.

If a business is a financial institution, then it should also release a statement of sources and uses of Qard[2] funds. This statement shows the amount of money that the institution has loaned without interest, and is structured to show the sources and uses of Qard funds. The sources of funds for this statement are funds from a bank's current account, funds from the bank's owners, and funds from transactions that were not compliant with Islamic law.

The overriding disclosure concept under Islamic law is that information disclosures should be accurate, complete, reliable, and free of bias. This is similar to the principles-based approach of IFRS, rather than the specific reporting requirements mandated by GAAP. Thus, someone using window dressing techniques to artificially enhance the reported results, financial position, or cash flows of a business would be going against Islamic law.

Islamic Accounting Principles

Most accounting principles under Islamic accounting do not vary from those promulgated under GAAP or IFRS accounting. In this section, we only note those areas in which there are differences.

Business transactions are recorded at their cost in Islamic accounting. Thus, the cost of goods purchased for later resale is recorded at their cost. However, Zakat is payable based on the market value of one's wealth, which calls for a separate appraisal of asset and liability values, using their current values. This means that, for the purpose of computing the Zakat liability, the balance sheet must be restated so that assets are reported at their current values.

It is essential to use the matching principle in Islamic accounting, where all costs associated with earned revenue are recognized in the same period when the revenue was recognized. This is needed in order to correctly determine the profits or losses generated from a transaction, which in turn is used to determine the wealth upon which Zakat payments are based.

Both the cash basis of accounting and the accrual basis of accounting are acceptable under Islamic accounting, though accrual accounting is preferred[3]. The cash basis of accounting is the practice of recording revenue when cash is received, and recording expenses when cash has been paid out. Conversely, the accrual basis of accounting is the practice of recording revenues when earned and expenses as incurred. Since there are timing differences between these approaches, the method adopted will have an impact on the amount of Zakat paid out in any given year.

---

[2] Qard refers to a benevolent loan. It may be extended on a goodwill basis, mainly for welfare purposes. Under Islamic law, unused funds should be loaned out without an interest obligation.

[3] For financial institutions, the use of the cash basis requires you to explain this in the accompanying footnotes, and provide a reconciliation to show the firm's financial position under the accrual basis of accounting.

A unique aspect of Islamic law is the concept of social accountability, where a business is obligated to report any information to which financial statement users are morally entitled. Disclosures are also mandated for the impact of an organization on society at large. We cover this issue at greater length shortly.

Sharia Auditing

Sharia auditing is an assessment of the extent to which Islamic financial institutions follow the principles and rules of Islamic law. The general concept is similar to the services provided by any external audit firm, but with a reoriented focus. The outcome of a Sharia audit is the issuance of an auditor's opinion about whether an organization's financial statements have been issued in accordance with Sharia principles and Islamic accounting standards.

Users of Islamic Accounting Information

The users of Islamic accounting information include the usual group that would peruse GAAP or IFRS financial statements – this group includes managers, employees, investors, governments, and creditors. In addition, Zakat authorities use this information to determine how accurately a business has calculated Zakat. Under Islamic law, reporting to society in general is more important than reporting to investors and creditors, which tends to skew the type of financial reporting that is issued in the direction of social impact.

Social Responsibility Reporting

Under the GAAP and IFRS accounting frameworks, the reporting emphasis has always been on the financial status of the reporting entity. This is by no means the case under Islamic accounting, where the disclosure of social and environmental information is considered to be at least as important as the disclosure of financial information. This is because the Quran states that the individual is the trustee of God's resources, and is expected to use those resources for the benefit of society as a whole.

There is no social responsibility framework that is specifically endorsed under Islamic law, so it is up to the reporting entity to adopt and follow one of the several frameworks that are available. A good example is the Global Reporting Initiative (GRI), which provides a detailed and exceedingly comprehensive itemization of the areas in which disclosures should be made, as well as the nature of those disclosures. The GRI disclosure structure is split up into three pieces, which are economic, environmental, and social. The general classifications of these GRI disclosures are as follows:

Economic:

- Anti-competitive behavior
- Anti-corruption
- Economic performance

- Indirect economic impacts
- Market presence
- Procurement practices
- Tax

Note: In addition to these categories of disclosures, an Islamic business might disclose the amount of Zakat it has paid, whether it engages in any forbidden activities, whether it engages in any interest-generating activities, and whether it acts as a monopoly in any of the markets it serves.

Environmental:

- Biodiversity
- Emissions
- Energy
- Environmental compliance
- Materials
- Supplier environmental assessment
- Waste
- Water and effluents

Social:

- Child labor
- Customer privacy
- Diversity and equal opportunity
- Employment
- Forced or compulsory labor
- Freedom of association and collective bargaining
- Human rights assessment
- Labor/management relations
- Local communities
- Marketing and labeling
- Non-discrimination
- Occupational health and safety
- Public policy, customer health and safety
- Rights of indigenous peoples
- Security practices
- Socioeconomic compliance
- Supplier social assessment
- Training and education

> **Note:** In addition to these categories of disclosures, an Islamic business might disclose whether a proper place of worship has been set aside for employees, and whether those employees are allowed to complete their obligatory prayers during the work day.

As an example of the types of disclosures that an Islamic business might issue that are linked to social responsibility reporting, we have included several extracts from a recent annual report of Saudi Aramco, the largest oil and gas company in the world. They are as follows:

> While the Company endeavors to have strong controls in place to mitigate the risk of operational incidents, five fatalities (one employee and four contractors) sadly occurred during the year. The Company and its operationally controlled entities also experienced 11 Tier 1 process safety events. Compared to the prior year, the total recordable case (TRC) frequency improved by 7.4% and the loss time injuries/illnesses (LTI) rate improved by 17.6%.

> The Company promotes and supports diversity and inclusion (D&I), occupational health, and mental well-being. Over the past five years, Aramco's commitment to D&I has resulted in the percentage of female hires increasing due to a concerted effort to achieve strategic targets and KPIs administered under a dedicated Diversity and Inclusion Division. There has been an increase of 22.6% for females in leadership positions at the Company [in the past year,] with strategic plans to continue on this upward trajectory. A major contributor to Aramco's success in boosting diversity has been the establishment of diversity and inclusion corporate targets, and KPIs on female representation, women in leadership, and people with disabilities representation...

> Aramco is implementing best practice environmental management systems and investing in initiatives that improve natural habitats and reduce damage to shared resources as the Company aspires to create a legacy for future generations. One of the ways this is achieved is by seeking to limit groundwater use in operations and protecting sensitive ecological areas to support Aramco's efforts to preserve the Kingdom's environment and any areas in which it operates. Headquartered in one of the most arid environments in the world, water management has been an essential focus of Aramco since inception.

> Aramco strives to achieve zero spills. There were 15 hydrocarbon spills in 2022 with two of the spills responsible for more than 99% of the total volume spilled. Eighty-nine percent of the contaminated soil related to one of the spills was removed to rehabilitate the affected area and further cleanup operations are ongoing. All of the spilled oil related to the second spill was recovered. The Company captures lessons learned from any hydrocarbon spill and shares them across its business. It also seeks to improve its spill prevention processes, asset integrity and inspection, response to hydrocarbon spill emergencies, and its hydrocarbon recovery processes...

> During the year, Aramco planted 11 million mangrove seedlings in-Kingdom, bringing the cumulative total to 24 million mangrove seedlings. The Company also completed the third phase of its million trees initiative, bringing the total number of native

trees planted in-Kingdom to three million. Mangroves have the capacity to act as carbon sinks, supporting the decarbonization plan. The replanting of mangrove coastlines supports increased biodiversity of fauna and flora. Aramco's biodiversity policy highlights the Company's aspiration to have a net positive impact on biodiversity across its operations.

Of particular interest in these disclosures is the company's willingness to divulge negative information, such as five deaths in the preceding year and 15 hydrocarbon spills. This approach shows a commitment to being forthright in revealing problem areas, where other members of society can see this information. It is unlikely that a Western company would reveal such information unless they were forced to do so. In addition, the discussion of mangrove seedlings, a major effort, shows the Islamic orientation toward activities that benefit the environment.

Summary

Islamic accounting generally following the IFRS accounting framework. However, it departs from this framework in a few key areas. One is certainly the reporting of balance sheet information in order to calculate Zakat. Another difference is in the modification of financial statements to incorporate Zakat liabilities and payments, as well as to generate a value-added statement, and to report the sources and uses of funds related to Zakat and charity payments. And a potentially major difference is the enhanced Islamic orientation toward social responsibility reporting, which can be much more extensive than what is required by the IFRS framework.

Glossary

H

Held for sale securities. Securities acquired with the intent of selling them in the short term for a profit.

M

Mudaraba. A form of partnership in which one party provides the capital while the other party provides labor, with both sharing in the profits.

N

Nisab. The lowest amount that a Muslim must possess to fulfill the Zakat obligation.

Q

Qard. A benevolent loan for which no interest payment is expected.

S

Sharia. The entirety of Islamic law, prescribing both religious and secular duties.

Special-purpose vehicle. A separate legal entity, used as a trustee to handle sukuk transactions under Islamic accounting.

Sukuk. An Islamic financial certificate.

Z

Zakat. An obligatory payment made annually under Islamic law on certain kinds of property and used for charitable and religious purposes.

Index

www.ingramcontent.com/pod-product-compliance
Lightning Source LLC
Chambersburg PA
CBHW051431200326
41520CB00023B/7436